Three Little Latin Rondos

for Flute and Piano
(2012)

By
Jon Jeffrey Grier

Piano Accompaniment

Program Notes

These are original stylized dances in three styles originating in Spanish-speaking regions of the Western Hemisphere. I. and II. are in 2nd rondo form (ABACA), and III. is in 3rd rondo (ABACBA). *Samba* is a Brazilian genre originating in the Afro-Brazilian communities of Rio de Janeiro in the early 20th century, with its roots in the cultural expressions of West Africa and in Brazilian folk traditions. It phrases in a steady, energetic duple meter with many syncopated subdivisions. The dance called the *tango* originated in poorer districts of Buenos Aires and Montevideo, with the music derived from the fusion of various forms of dance music from Europe and some possible influence from the *habanera*. *Calypso* is an Afro-Caribbean genre that originated in Trinidad and Tobago during the early to the mid-19th century and spread to the rest of the Caribbean Antilles and Venezuela by the mid-20th century. Its rhythms can be traced back to the arrival of French planters and their slaves from the French Antilles in the 18th century. It is characterized by a lively tempo and generally short insistent phrases; lyrics are sometimes humorous.

About the Composer

Jon Jeffrey Grier holds a B.A. from Kalamazoo College, where he studied composition with Lawrence Rackley, an M.M. in Composition from Western Michigan University, studying with Ramon Zupko, and an M.M. in Theory and a D.M.A. in Composition from the University of South Carolina, where he studied with Jerry Curry, Dick Goodwin and Sam Douglas. Jon taught Advanced Placement Music Theory and Music History at the Greenville Fine Arts Center, a magnet school of the arts in Greenville, SC from 1988 to 2019, where he was named Teacher of the Year three times. Awards include grants from ASCAP, the Surdna Foundation, the South Carolina Music Teachers Association, the Metropolitan Arts Council, and the Atlanta Chamber Players. Jon has also been a writer/keyboardist in various jazz & fusion ensembles since 1984. He lives in Greenville with wife Marion and Carolina Dingo Roxanne.

THREE LITTLE LATIN RONDOS

I. Una Samba Seria

Jon Jeffrey Grier

50410007

4

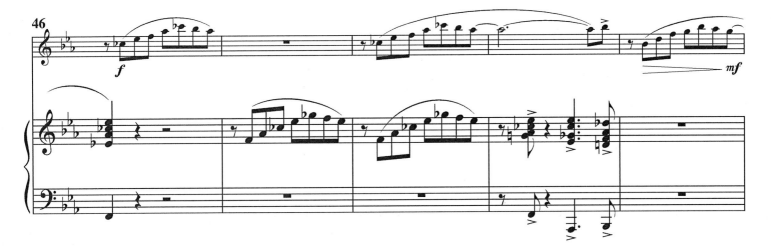

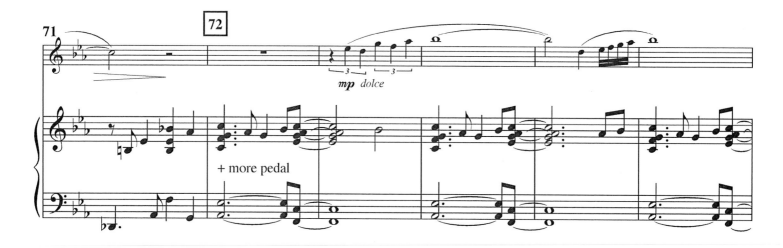

II. Tango de la Noche

Poco misterioso ♩ = 96

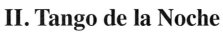

Three Little Latin Rondos

for Flute and Piano
(2012)

By
Jon Jeffrey Grier

Flute

Flute

THREE LITTLE LATIN RONDOS

I. Una Samba Seria

Jon Jeffrey Grier

50410007

4

II. Tango de la Noche

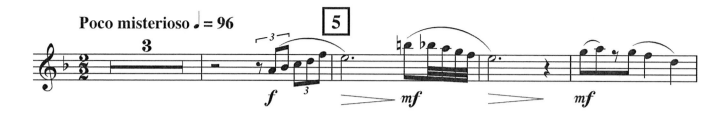

50410007

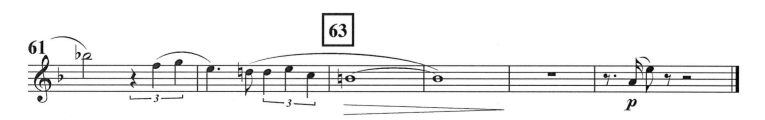

50410007

III. ¡Carnaval!

Program Notes

These are original stylized dances in three styles originating in Spanish-speaking regions of the Western Hemisphere. I. and II. are in 2nd rondo form (ABACA), and III. is in 3rd rondo (ABACBA). *Samba* is a Brazilian genre originating in the Afro-Brazilian communities of Rio de Janeiro in the early 20th century, with its roots in the cultural expressions of West Africa and in Brazilian folk traditions. It phrases in a steady, energetic duple meter with many syncopated subdivisions. The dance called the *tango* originated in poorer districts of Buenos Aires and Montevideo, with the music derived from the fusion of various forms of dance music from Europe and some possible influence from the *habanera*. *Calypso* is an Afro-Caribbean genre that originated in Trinidad and Tobago during the early to the mid-19th century and spread to the rest of the Caribbean Antilles and Venezuela by the mid-20th century. Its rhythms can be traced back to the arrival of French planters and their slaves from the French Antilles in the 18th century. It is characterized by a lively tempo and generally short insistent phrases; lyrics are sometimes humorous.

About the Composer

Jon Jeffrey Grier holds a B.A. from Kalamazoo College, where he studied composition with Lawrence Rackley, an M.M. in Composition from Western Michigan University, studying with Ramon Zupko, and an M.M. in Theory and a D.M.A. in Composition from the University of South Carolina, where he studied with Jerry Curry, Dick Goodwin and Sam Douglas. Jon taught Advanced Placement Music Theory and Music History at the Greenville Fine Arts Center, a magnet school of the arts in Greenville, SC from 1988 to 2019, where he was named Teacher of the Year three times. Awards include grants from ASCAP, the Surdna Foundation, the South Carolina Music Teachers Association, the Metropolitan Arts Council, and the Atlanta Chamber Players. Jon has also been a writer/keyboardist in various jazz & fusion ensembles since 1984. He lives in Greenville with wife Marion and Carolina Dingo Roxanne.

III. ¡Carnaval!

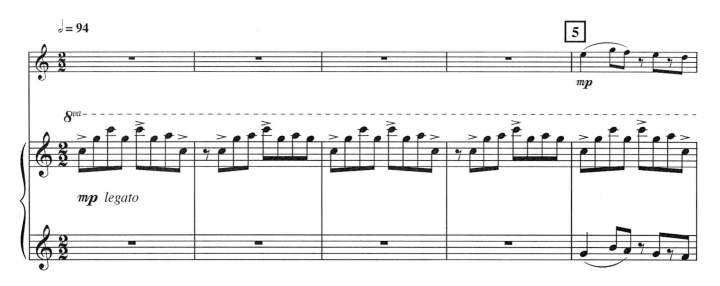

50410007

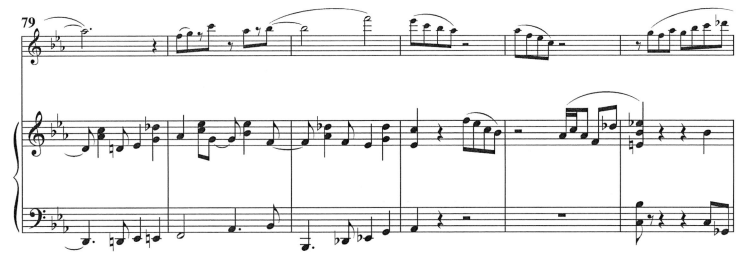

Selected Flute Publications

METHODS

BAKER, JULIUS
Cox, Alan

10300130   Daily Exercises for the Flute (Grade 4)
A terrific and valuable collection of exercises for advanced flutists, the studies in this book are intended to build a high degree of technical solidity by means of intensive work on scale, scale patterns, seventh-chord progressions, thirds, sixths, chromatic sequences, fast staccato, high tones, and various duet selections. By diligent and careful work on these daily exercises, students will build a flawless tehcnical foundation on the flute, and more advanced players will keep themselves in shape.

COLLECTIONS

BALENT, ANDREW

50341003   Classical Solos (Grade 2.5)

HARRIS, FLOYD O.

50341006   Competition Solos, Book 3 Flute (Grade 3.5)
A practical collection of competition solos for young instrumentalists, many of which are on state festival lists. The piano book includes alternate accompaniments for instruments of different pitch and therefore can be used for any instrument in the book three series. Titles included: Brass Bangles; Caprice; Dancing Silhouettes; Evening in the Country; Ocean Beach (Valse); Polka from Bartered Bride; Viennese Sonata No. 4 (Rondo)

HARRIS, FLOYD/ SIENNICKI, EDMUND

50341005   Competition Solos, Book 2 Flute/Oboe (Grade 2.5)
Book 2 is a practical collection of competition solos, many of which are on state festival lists. Piano book includes alternate accompaniments for instruments of different pitch and therefore can be used for any instrument in the book two series. Titles included: The Young Prince; Viennese Sonatina No. 1 (Allegro); Flower of the Orient; The King's Jester; Two Short Pieces; Spirit of Victory; Barcarolle and Scherzetto; Sparkles; Waltz from Album for the Young.

KERKORIAN, GREGORY M.

50341008   Easy Orginal Flutes Duets and Trios
Beautifully written and arranged with the young player in mind, these duets and trios make wonderful concert and festival repertoire for early performance.

SOLO, UNACCOMPANIED

ADLER, SAMUEL

10410523   Canto XIII for Flute (Grade 4)
Adler, Samuel. Published by Ludwig Music, Cleveland,. Copyright 1994. A rare piece for solo piccolo, this work may be performed straight, or the player may make dramatic entrances and theatrical gestures.

FERROUD, PIERRE OCTAVE

M284891   Three Pieces

SIENNICKI, EDMUND J.

10340101   Recorder Fun (Grade 1)

SOLO WITH PIANO

BACH, J.S.
Marteau, Henri

10410234   Andante Cantabile (Grade 3)
Andante Cantabile [Sinfonia Concertante in E-flat for Two Violins and Orchestra: Andante]

BRICCIALDI, GIULIO
Davis, Albert O.

10410186   Carnival of Venice for Flute and Piano (Grade 4)
This famous melody in theme-and-variations form features a marvelous cadenza. Its technical challenges are dazzlingly impressive!

BUSSER, HENRI

M114291   Petite Suite

M298091   Prelude Et Scherzo

CASELLA, ALFREDO

M266891   Barcarola E Scherzo

M371291   Sicilienne and Burlesque

CHAMINADE, CECILE

M114791   Air De Ballet: Seren

DEBUSSY, CLAUDE

M168591   Clair De Lune

GANNE, LOUIS

M127091   Andante Et Scherzo

GAUBERT, PHILIPPE

M186691   Deux Esquisses

M122791   Nocturne Et Allegro

M196191   Sicilienne: Madrigal

M218391   Sonata In A

M297991   Suite (Grade 4)
This suite, by renowned French flutist Philippe Gaubert, is in four movements, with each movement dedicated to a master flutist of the time. It is a fine contest or recital selection for the advancing musician. Movements: I. Invocation (danse de pretresses), II. Berceuse Orientale, III. Barcarolle, IV. Shzerzo-Valse

GERMAN, EDWARD

M330491   Suite

GLIERE, REINHOLD

M330691   Two Pieces, Op.35

GRIFFES, CHARLES TOMLINSON

M282291   Poeme

HAHN, REYNALDO

M342491   Two Pieces

HARTY, HAMILTON

M292591   In Ireland

HUE, GEORGES

M152191   Fantaisie (Grade 4)
Composed for the Paris Conservatory 1913 and later orchestrated in 1923, Hue's Fantaisie is a beautiful work for the advancing flutist. The piece begins with a spacious and atmospheric Assez lent section, which is complimented by intricate melodic lines on the flute. This introduction leads into a beautiful Modere section and concludes with a rousing Tres vif encore.

REINECKE, CARL

W100891   Concerto Op. 283

ROSENHAUS, STEVEN

P001791   Rescuing Psyche
Rescuing Psyche for flute and piano was commissioned by the Music Teachers National Association and the NYSTMA and was premiered by flutist Kelly J. Covert and pianist Nathan Hess. Rescuing Psyche takes its inspiration from Greek mythology. Eros, a god, and Psyche, a mortal, are in love, but Aphrodite is jealous. Aphrodite successfully traps the mortal in a coma, but Eros wakes his love by playing a flute. The flute part has some key clicks and flutters but no other extended techniques or special effects are required.

WIDOR, CHARLES-MARIE

M183591   Suite, Op. 34

TRIO

KOECHLIN, CHARLES

M333291   Three Divertissements

Exclusively Distributed by

Questions/ comments? info@keisersouthernmusic.com